THE EDUCATION
OF
CHRIST
Hillside Reveries

THE EDUCATION OF CHRIST

Hillside Reveries

WILLIAM MITCHELL RAMSAY, D. C. L.

Introduction by EDWARD M. BLAIKLOCK
Illustrations by RON McCARTY

Keats Publishing, Inc. ✠ New Canaan, Connecticut

THE EDUCATION OF CHRIST

Shepherd Illustrated Classic Edition published 1981

Special contents of this edition copyright © 1981 by
Keats Publishing, Inc.

Library of Congress Catalog Card Number: 80-84438
ISBN: 0-87983-236-3

Printed in the United States of America

SHEPHERD ILLUSTRATED CLASSICS are published by
Keats Publishing, Inc.,
36 Grove Street, New Canaan, Connecticut 06840

CONTENTS

ILLUSTRATIONS

INTRODUCTION TO THE SHEPHERD ILLUSTRATED CLASSICS EDITION

I am pleased, in writing some words of introduction to this book, to bear testimony to the influence William Mitchell Ramsay has had for half a century on my own New Testament studies. I discovered him back in the thirties, when, as a young University teacher in Classics and Ancient History, I was becoming preoccupied with a theme which was to be dominant in what I have written and said on the New Testament, the unity of ancient Greek literature.

The New Testament is an enormously valuable collection of first century documents. Classical historians generally have neglected the fact to their loss, until recently. Where else, save in the most restricted corners, can they find the common people, life in a turbulent Roman province on the Empire's outer edge, the patterns of social life and government in Greek and Roman communities in the first generations of the Roman Peace, the global activities of the Jews, citizenship, colonial status, free cities, the pagan cults? In fact, little Greek and Roman writing survives from the years over which, in history and epistle, the New Testament spreads its documented evidence. Under some myopic spell the historians neglected the whole collection.

Ramsay deepened, expanded and informed the conviction which was shaping in my own early study. As Professor of Humanity (or Classics) at Aberdeen for a generation (1886 to 1911) he was one of my own tribe. He had discovered in his archaeological work in Asia Minor the supreme worth of Luke, in his own right to be regarded one of the leading historians of the Greeks. The role of archaeology and geography in the study of history was also becoming clear to me in both the spheres of Classical scholarship and New Testament. Ramsay majors on this.

My own career and early research had long since convinced me that the only safe approach to the study of the New Testament, its literary and historical criticism, was by way of the Classics, and a sound knowledge of Greek, Latin and imperial history. How much nonsense in the realm of New Testament studies would have remained unwritten, had New Testament scholars brought to the study of its half century of documents, the canons and discipline taken for granted by the classicist and a wide view of the history of its times. Hence the enthusiasm with which I began to collect Ramsay's books: *The Historical Geography of Asia Minor* (1890), *The Church in the Roman Empire* (1893), *Saint Paul, the Traveller and Roman Citizen* and the rest.

Ramsay died in 1939 in his late eighties, but long before then he had made his point with me. My own small contributions to his tradition will all reveal my debt. Archaeology, geography and the literature of Greece and Rome are the visible ingredients of all I have had to say on the New Testament. They have all been sources of immense enlightenment and understanding. The story of Christ at Nazareth, above the great view of the history-laden Esdraelon Plain, is illustration, in the present volume, of the understanding I have in mind.

The deep interest, of course, in the staunch conservatism of Ramsay's New Testament scholarship, is that it

began very far from conservatism. The reckless con
clusions of German-born liberalism were almost uni
versally accepted when Ramsay, curiously unfitted for
the task, took up his researches in Asia Minor. It was
the stark compulsion of facts upon the ground which
impressed the truth of relevant passages from the Acts
of the Apostles upon his mind—a mind fundamentally
honest and classically trained. The world of biblical
scholarship has paid dearly for the wild speculations of
nineteenth century Germany. To Ramsay, the world
will always be indebted for the beginnings of the vast
salvage operation this century has seen.

Scholars travel now. They must. They see the sites
of history. The science of archaeology has matured.
The requirements of the German Ph.D. degree are no
longer thought the path to learning. Conservative
scholarship is on its feet. Ramsay was one of the first to
show it where to go.

The present volume, as the Preface narrates, is the
result of a perceptive visit to the Holy Land in 1902. Its
pages will serve as an introduction to the man, and his
insight into that strong interweaving of place and time,
of stage and circumstance, which were part of his
contribution to ancient studies. They will never be
separated again.

Edward M. Blaiklock
February 1981

PREFACE

IN a form much abbreviated to suit the due limits, Chapters I.-V. and VIII. of this book formed the Murtle Lecture in the University of Aberdeen, on 2nd February, 1902.

The lecture—not really a lecture, but rather the dream of a student's life—was given only with reluctance and much diffidence, in deference to the wishes of those who are responsible for the lectures. It is published now, in an improved but still imperfect form, at the wish of my friend Dr. Robertson Nicoll (from whose advice I have on other occasions gained much), in the hope that, such as it is, it may be not altogether devoid of interest for a wider audience, if such it should find.

The pertinence and, one might almost say, the necessity of the additions, Prologue and Chapters VI.-VII., will probably be evident to every reader.

It is right to add that part of the first chapter is taken with slight modification from a paper read before the Royal Geographical Society in London, 10th March, 1902, on the influence of geographical conditions on the history and religion of Asia Minor (to be published in the *Geographical Journal*, September, 1902), also that Chapters III. and V. are adapted and improved from a paper contributed at the request and suggestion of my friend the editor, Mr. C. G. Trumbull of

PREFACE

Philadelphia, U.S., to the *Sunday School Times*, 10th February, 1900, on the influence which the surroundings of Nazareth exercised on the mind of Christ.

To avoid criticism it may be explained, that though for brevity's sake I have spoken of Nain as if it were on the site of the modern village at the foot of the hill, yet there can be little doubt that the ancient city was on the top. If I may express an opinion, Nain seems to have more claim than Safed, which is probably a purely modern town, to be the "city set on a hill".

W. M. RAMSAY.

KING'S COLLEGE,
ABERDEEN, 1*st Sept.* 1902.

PROLOGUE

THE POWER OF THE GREAT PLAINS

PROLOGUE.

THE POWER OF THE GREAT PLAINS.

IN view of the high importance which in the following pages is attributed to natural surroundings and geographical conditions as an educative influence on the mind of Jesus and on all mankind—an importance which some may consider exaggerated—it seems right to incorporate in this preliminary chapter some justificatory and explanatory remarks, and to draw them from the writer's own experience. It is only fair to make clear in the beginning the prepossessions—it may be prejudices —which are inherent in the ensuing chapters, especially as they contain, not any formal argument or exposition, but merely the impressions and dreams of an individual.

For example, the writer takes the view in a later chapter that the unresponsiveness of

Renan's mind to the interest and historic grandeur of Jerusalem was a natural concomitant and symptom of his inability to comprehend the width of outlook and of sympathy that characterised Jesus : accordingly the great French scholar's picture of that *âme tendre et délicate du Nord* remains a sentimental fancy and never approaches historic reality. Had his intellect been free to respond sympathetically to the spirit of the country, he would have seen the life and understood the spirit of Jesus differently ; but he began to study with alienated sympathies, and could see neither rightly.

Such a criticism may be condemned as springing from mere prejudice. Doubtless many will consider that so learned, *spirituel* and eloquent a scholar as Renan must have been able to judge Jerusalem aright, and that one who does not possess a tithe of Renan's knowledge of its history ought not to presume to criticise his capacities and his work. Those who judge thus would not be likely to agree with the views which are stated in the following chapters, if they should read them.

Yet those prepossessions—or prejudices—are but a slow growth.

I look back on the reading of Renan's *Vie de Jésus* in early college days as one of the great pleasures of my youth, and am grateful to that brilliant writer for stimulation of intellect and new thoughts.   Anything that I say in criticism is only the outcome of more than thirty years of meditation about questions which were in my mind when I read the book, and have never been long absent, but have kept recurring during watches by night and work by day, on land and on sea. As I pondered over the problems of Anatolian history and topography, during long marches over the plains of Lycaonia and Cappadocia, or in riding from village to village over the bare, gently swelling hills of Phrygia, those other questions kept their place and claimed attention.   Ideas which began in the reading of T. H. Green's *Witness of God*, while I was reading for the Final Schools in Oxford, gradually shaped and remodelled and re-arranged themselves; and at last were compacted and cemented in the educative experience of a ten days' ride from Damascus to Jerusalem.

Most of all it has been the experience of the impressive vastness and uniformity and unvaryingness, monotone not monotonous, of the Central Anatolian plateau that has influenced the thoughts here expressed. It is impossible for any one to live or to travel long in those level solitudes without having his mind and thought profoundly affected by them. The strange and indescribable charm which they exert on every explorer will be attested by many, who may not share in all the views which I express.

Some people are more sensitive than others to the influence of those impressive solitudes. The power that lives in them speaks to men in different ways; but it influences—whether they are conscious of it or not—all men and all nations that come within its range. To those who are accustomed to gain their knowledge of the world through observation of natural phenomena, mainly by the eye, that power will address itself through the eye. To those whose life is spent in thinking over problems of history and philosophy and scholarship it will reveal itself accordingly. But when you attempt to define or express the subtle influence that the great plains exercise, it eludes description and defies analysis. You see it in history ; you become aware of it in life ; but you cannot seize it.

I must turn to the form of literature in which some of the deepest thought and most acute observation of nature at the present time seeks expression—prose fiction—in order to find an attempt to give body to the spirit of which I speak. Some years ago I was struck with the vivid yet delicate sensitiveness to the life and power of nature, shown in the following paragraphs of a story by Mr. Owen Rhoscomyl, the scene of which was laid on the Western Prairies of America. They expressed what I had long been in search of, and what I had found no other writer to express.

Appearing in the lightest pages of one of the lightest popular magazines of the day, the Christmas number of the *Idler*, in some year about 1895, the story, grim and realistic, stood out very impressively from its somewhat frivolous surroundings, as the brief, compact utterance of a life's experience. One felt immediately that the author had lived in the scene of his story, and that the paragraphs which are quoted in the following pages contained no fanciful fiction, but were transcribed from the book of reality.

I was at the time groping to find analogies in the ordinary life of the common average man to the experience of St. Paul, when *as he was come nigh unto Damascus, there shined round about him a light from heaven, above the brightness of the sun.* In Mr. Rhoscomyl's paragraphs I seemed to listen to the account of such an incident.   The author was known to me only as the writer of romances about Wales and Welshmen ; but I recognised at once that he must have lived for years on the plains, in order to become so saturated with their spirit as to give it such free and compressed utterance.   Taking the liberty of writing to him, I learned that my impression as to the life and experience of the writer, and as to the intention and meaning of the paragraphs, was entirely correct, and that the analogy, which I had caught as I read, was in the author's thoughts as he wrote ; and he kindly permitted me to make use of his words for my purpose.

One must remember that the incident described in the paragraphs which follow is not taken from the life of a sentimental or excitable race, but from the experience of a class, who are as cool, hardy, self-reliant and reckless as any men in the world—the cowboys of the Prairies.

Two days ago he was riding back, alone,

in the afternoon, from an unsuccessful search after strayed horses, and suddenly, all in the lifting of a hoof, the weird prairie had gleamed into eerie life, had dropped the veil and spoken to him; while the breeze stopped, and the sun stood still for a flash in waiting for his answer. And he, his heart in a grip of ice, the frozen flesh a-crawl with terror upon his loosened bones, white-lipped and wide-eyed with frantic fear, uttered a yell of horror as he dashed the spurs into his panic-stricken horse, in a mad endeavour to escape from the Awful Presence that filled all earth and sky from edge to edge of vision.

Then, almost in the same flash, the unearthly light died out of the dim prairie, the veil swept across into place again; and he managed to check his wild flight, and look about him. His empty lips were jibbering without a sound escaping them, and his very heart shivered with cold, for all the brassy heat of the day. But the breeze was wandering on again; under the great sun the prairie spread dim to the south-

west, and tawny to the north-east; only between his own loose knees the horse trembled in every limb, and mumbled the bit with dry mouth. All was as before in earth and sky, apparently, but not in his own self. It was as if his spirit stood apart from him, putting questions which he could not answer, and demanding judgment upon problems which he dare not reason out.

Then he remembered what this thing was which had happened. The prairie had spoken to him, as sooner or later it spoke to most men that rode it. It was a something well known amongst them, but known without words, and as by a subtle instinct, for no man who had experienced it ever spoke willingly about it afterwards. Only the man would be changed; some began to be more reckless, as if a dumb blasphemy rankled hidden in their breasts. Others, coming with greater strength perhaps to the ordeal, became quieter, looking squarely at any danger as they faced it, but continuing ahead as though quietly confident that nothing happened save as the gods ordained.

If I consulted the author, it was not that
I needed any confirmation of my first impression, or any assurance that this passage is no
fanciful piece of fiction, like the introduction
of ghostly apparitions, and strange premoni-
tions, and the rest of the stock-in-trade of
the ordinary story-teller.   One recognises the
spirit of the great level plains in that remarkable effort of description, just as certainly as,
when one stands

> Where the long green reed-beds sway
> In the rippled waters grey
> Of that solitary lake
> Where Mæander's springs are born ;
> Where the ridged pine-wooded roots
> Of Messogis westward break,

and reads the various descriptions given of
that famous scene by different authors, one
knows that Strabo had been there, but that
neither Herodotus nor Matthew Arnold had
ever seen the spot, and one recognises what
Arnold has gathered from Strabo.   But you
need reasons and external authority before you

can state to the world what you know with inward certainty.

The physical effects which the author describes are, of course, special to the individual, in whom deep feeling finds outward expression after the fashion that belongs to his own idiosyncrasy. So, too, the perception of the influence is accomplished through the sense of sight, but this also is an accident of the individual temperament. The reality of the phenomenon consists in the consciousness, too suddenly awakened, of the Divine nature that lives in the vast world around him. He has seen, and he knows, as by one of those *flashes struck from midnights*, those *fire-flames noondays kindle*, those *moments*

> Sure though seldom,
> When the spirit's true endowments
> Stand out plainly from its false ones.

The Divine power has manifested itself to him, and he can never again lose the knowledge, nor live the unthinking and free life of former days. That consciousness, from which he can never escape, which he cannot doubt or disown before his own soul, is a power within him, driving him on to his destined fate. He struggles against it, and rebels; but it is all in vain.

Not essentially dissimilar are the terms in which Virgil describes Apollo's prophetess, terms somewhat fanciful, but modelled on some older account of the prophetic frenzy :—

> And as before the doors in view
> She stands, her visage pales its hue,
> Her locks dishevelled fly,
> Her breath comes thick, her wild heart glows,
> Dilating as the madness grows,
> As breathing nearer and more near
> The God comes rushing on his seer.
> The seer impatient of control
> Raves in the cavern vast,
> And madly struggles from her soul
> The incumbent power to cast :
> He, mighty Master, plies the more
> Her foaming mouth, all chafed and sore,
> Tames her wild heart with plastic hand,
> And makes her docile to command.

The agony, the struggle and the suffering spring from the resistance of the untutored, half-savage soul to the Divine message. Far different is it with a nature like that which animated the great Hebrew prophets, to which the Divine message comes as the welcome longed-for guide of a soul in search of it, already educated into eagerness to listen and to obey.

What must especially be emphasised is that in this case, which Mr. Rhoscomyl has portrayed as a typical and representative one, the physical experience, the affection of the sense of sight, which forms the method of manifestation, is no mere trivial or fanciful misinterpretation of the phenomena of nature. It is the outward concomitant of the soul's perception, in a case where the soul cannot be reached without some such impression of the senses. The man cannot grasp the idea except through the senses, and especially the sense of sight, in which all his work and life have moved. He has been accustomed to live by the eye, to trust to it, to stake his life daily on its quickness and certainty, to learn almost

exclusively through it. Nothing can sufficiently impress him with its reality except
through the sight. But his eye is as quick
and true as the eagle's. He knows that it can
make no mistake : no more than a woodman
can mistake an oak for an elm : what it shows
him is for him real.

But to describe what he has seen, and to
make another understand how he has gained
his knowledge, there lies the impossible.
The best that can be done in the way of
description, either in the case of Saul or of
that Prairie rider, will always seem to many to
contain an element of diseased and fanciful
error.

But those who have known know. What
seems to be distempered in the language arises
only from the inadequacy of human expression
to paint the truth. Every description must
make use of metaphor and analogy and sensuous imagery to express what is essentially
above the level of ordinary experience. Hence
all such attempts at expression must be read

with sympathetic understanding and with a firm resolution not to bind down the meaning to the exact and strict limits of the imperfect terms which are employed.

When the Divine power manifests itself to man, he knows it, and it becomes to him a possession for ever, to rule in him or to destroy him : there is no middle way. When it has revealed itself to others, we recognise the truth by its effect on them ; but we cannot understand in what way the Divine truth has revealed itself to them, nor can they explain the process to us.

But only the arrogant self-satisfaction, which makes one's own narrow range of power and knowledge the measure of all things, which disbelieves and derides everything in another that is unfamiliar to oneself, will depreciate the experience which is dimly and figuratively described in the words just quoted.

Although, however, the individual case eludes us, and mocks all attempt to under-stand or to measure it, we can trace this influence more certainly and picture it more definitely in the history of a race, through the accumulating experience of generations ; for every country has its special character, and influences its inhabitants in its own way.

In Anatolia, on the vast plains of the Central Plateau, we have a country which shows considerable analogy to, along with certain differences from, that where the paragraphs which have been quoted found their origin. On those great level plains the spirit of man seems to be separated from the world by the mountains which shut it off from the sea, and thus to be thrown back on its own nature ; but it is not confined, for the idea of confinement is absolutely alien to that vast expanse, where the sole limit to the range of the human eye seems to be its own weakness of vision, where a distant mountain-peak only emphasises the sense of vastness, inasmuch as it furnishes a standard by which to estimate distance. The great eye of heaven, unwearying, unchanging, inexorable, watches you from

its rising over the level horizon till it sinks
below the same level again. You breathe an
atmosphere of inevitable acquiescence in the
Infinite Power which is around you, all-
pervasive and compelling. The sense of
individuality and personal power grows weak
and shrinks away, not daring to show itself in
the human consciousness.

The phases of the year co-operate in this
effect, with a long severe winter and a shorter
but hot summer. Where water pours forth
in one of the many great springs which give
birth to strong-flowing rivers, the country is
a garden ; but otherwise the fertile soil is
dependent entirely on the chances of an
uncertain rainfall, unless man follows the
teaching of the ancient Anatolian religion
and practises irrigation. The steadily blow-
ing north wind tempers the heat, and the
harvester trusts to it with perfect confidence
to winnow his grain on the threshing-floor.

Everything impresses on the mind the utter
insignificance of man, and his absolute de-

pendence on the Divine power and the Divine teaching. The peasant of the present day still calls every great life-giving spring "God-hath-given" (*Huda-Verdi*).

But the Divine power that was so evident was not the stern, pitiless power of the hard desert. The desert can inspire in man only resignation before the fate which is always overhanging him but always incalculable, which he can neither guard against nor prepare for, but must accept when it comes upon him. Islam with its fatalistic acquiescence is the growth that must spring from the desert.

The Anatolian people saw the nature of the land, rich and full of good things to those who accepted the divinely revealed method, and cared for the holy soil and the sacred animals, as the goddess, their mother and patron, required. St. Paul, with his usual unerring insight into the character of his audience, spoke to the rude Lycaonian peasants about the God " *who did good, and gave rain from heaven, and fruitful seasons, filling the heart with food and gladness*".

Hence sprang a religion of patience and docility, but a religion of work, not of dumb acquiescence in presence of an inevitable and unknowable fate. The reward could be calculated on. The order of nature could be understood, and man could adapt himself to it : the way was mapped out for him in the prescriptions of a religion which had fashioned itself for him in the country. It was a religion of peace and toil, of obedience and plasticity, which might have developed to higher forms in a state of continued peace ; but the country lay in the track of armies.

One feature in the Anatolian religion rises before us prominent and characteristic at the first glance. The custom familiar in other countries is that God is called the Father of all mankind and all life. Such is the almost universal European and Semitic expression. But it was the motherhood of the Divine nature that was the great feature in the

Anatolian worship.   The male element in the
Divine nature was recognised only as an
occasional and subsidiary actor in the drama
of nature and of life.   The life of man came
from the great Mother ; the heroes of the
land were the sons of the goddess, and at
death they returned to the mother who bore
them.   It was the Mother Goddess who
nourished her people, guided them through
life, taught them how to cultivate her land
and to breed and train her sacred animals to
their use, and at last received them back to
herself.

   In the history of the land the same impression remains : it is everywhere the most
pathetic of histories.   Not vigour and initia-
tive, but receptivity and impressibility, swayed
the spirit of the people, marked their fate, and
breathed through the atmosphere that sur-
rounded them—a continuous, barely perceptible force acting on every new people, and
subtly influencing every new religion, that
came into the land.   For example, the

earliest known trace of the veneration of the
Virgin Mary in the Christian religion is in a
Phrygian inscription of the second century;
and the earliest example of a holy place con-
secrated to the Mother of God as already an
almost Divine personality is at Ephesus early
in the fifth century.

For the student of the country and history,
it is always necessary to go back to that
religious susceptibility, to recognise it as the
originator of all racial life and of all social
forms, and as a continuous force acting
throughout the development of the country.
He observes, point by point, and detail
after detail, the natural characteristics of soil
and climate giving form and content to the
religious myths and beliefs and institutions
of the inhabitants, in spite of all outward
changes.

In the city of Ephesus an example may be
found of this principle.   Mr. Wood spent six
years searching for the site of the Temple of
Artemis, and at last he found it exactly where

it ought to be, a mile north-east from the
Greek city, beside the little hill on the top
of which was built the great church of St.
John, and on the lowest slope of which still
stands the splendid old mosque of Isa Bey.
The historical process is obvious, since Mr.
Wood's discovery disclosed it. The dominant
Christian religion had to claim for itself the
sanctity attaching to the ancient site, and it did
so by building that great church overlooking
the temple. But Christianity gave place to
Mohammedanism, and again this new religion
made itself heir to the religious associations
and holiness of the locality by constructing
between the two older religious sites one of
the largest and most splendid mosques in the
whole country.

In the history of Ephesus and in the history
of the whole country there is never any continuity either national or municipal, no unity
of racial or religious development. The one
thread of continuity consists in the religious
susceptibility, which the scene and atmosphere

of the land implant in man. That state of
feeling is far more deeply seated than creed or
ceremonial : it is, as it were, the half-articulate
substratum on which religion may be built up.
But it has found no development from within :
it has only been modified under impulses from
without. It has remained almost wholly in-
articulate and elementary; but still it remains,
hardly varying under many successive religious
forms, exercising no inconsiderable influence
even on Islam, which is itself too elementary
to be easily modified ; and it always attracts
the popular awe and reverence to the same
holy places, which were recognised thousands
of years ago as those where man came nearest
to, and was most readily influenced by, God.
Cities grow up and decay and are replaced by
new cities on new sites, which in their turn
pass into ruin as changes of sea-shore and
river-course alter the conditions that favour
municipal prosperity ; but the Divine never
changes, and its favoured abodes remain the
same.

A power like that, originating freely and spontaneously in the nature of the country, and breathed in its atmosphere, must be essentially right and true. Though it may be imperfectly understood by man, it is the Divine voice : it is a revelation of the Divine nature. What it has lacked is the opportunity of development. The historian will study the reasons and the causes ; but the fact is obvious that there has been only a process of degeneration, that the first stage was best, that the revelation stopped almost at its beginning. The changes that have occurred have been forced from without, not springing freely from the inner conditions. There has been no succession of seers to hear the Divine voice with increasing clearness and completeness ; but there has been a succession through the ages of invaders, of barbarous armies sweeping over the country, of foreign conquest and domination, of forced immigration ; there has been a frequently recurring state of uncertainty and danger, of helpless exposure to irresistible attack and massacre ; and these causes have prevented the needed formation and strengthening of national character, while they have frequently introduced foreign religions in the debased form in which the superstitious minds of a brutal and undisciplined Oriental soldiery could conceive them.

Religion to be true must be constantly growing. It cannot become stagnant without falsifying itself. The nation which does not increase in its power of interpreting the Divine purpose, and fails to produce a succession of listeners to and interpreters of the Divine voice, has become dead to the Divine message. In that country, where a true national character has never been allowed scope to develop, the history of religion has been one of degradation and of increase in the polytheistic spirit, which constitutes an infallible index of growing insensibility to the Divine nature. You learn there more clearly than in any other country that religion cannot be real and permanent except through the continuous revelation of the Divine nature to man.

That is the general principle which years of study have shown me as ruling in the history of the land. And, if it rules in the people, that is because it affects first of all the individual man.

CHAPTER I

ON A MOUNTAIN TOP

CHAPTER I.

ON A MOUNTAIN TOP.

IN the outset of the public career of Jesus stands the remarkable incident of the Temptation. The authority obviously is the account given of it by Himself to the disciples ; and we are told that " *without a parable spake He not to them* ". How far the details partake of the nature of parable, intended to make transcendental truth intelligible to the simple fishermen, we cannot precisely tell, and no man ought to dogmatise.

But no one doubts—no one can doubt— as to the essential truth that lies under the narrative.

Jesus had begun His life ignorant of His nature and His destiny, an unthinking infant. He had " *grown in wisdom and stature* ".

He had gradually attained, in thirty years of
education, in work and in thought, to a clear
conception of His mission, of the career that
lay before Him and its ultimate issue. Such
a career can be entered on only by one who
has fully weighed it all, and counted the cost,
and voluntarily, deliberately, with his eyes
open, taken on him the burden of that great
and terrible life and death.

During that period in which Jesus was contemplating in the solitude of the desert the
life that lay before Him, an alternative presented itself to His mind, and engaged His
attention for a time, and exercised a certain
attraction on Him, but was decisively rejected.
He was tempted to swerve from the career
which He had chosen ; but His firm resolve
proved superior to the temptation.

Jesus afterwards related the story to His
followers in such language as they could understand. It is surely alien to His nature to
suppose that He imparted this narrative to
them in order to show how infinitely superior

He was to the temptations that beset ordinary men, and how far the motives which appealed to them were from exercising any attraction on Him. An incident narrated in that spirit could only show that He stood far aloof from the difficulties and trials of common men.

Surely the purpose is plain in that story. Jesus felt the force of temptation, and it needed a distinct effort of will and resolution for Him to resist it. He was placed in a position where a real choice between alternative courses had to be made.

Those who were placed very near Him and in actual contact with His immediate followers, recognised that truth. As the writer of the Epistle to the Hebrews has said, " *He Himself hath suffered being tempted* " : He " *hath been in all points tempted like as we are,*" and hence He " *can be touched with the feeling of our weaknesses* ".

Nor can it be imagined that this was the first and only time when Jesus felt the attraction of some other possible career in life

Temptation does not come only once to a man; nor did it come only once to the Son of Man. But to every man of strong character there comes the last temptation—when the alternative which has been attracting him away from his true career is decisively rejected, and ceases for ever to tempt him. A great step in the development of his character is then achieved. Other difficulties may and will beset him, but that one weakness at least has been transformed into strength.

This final Temptation is the one which has been recorded for us at the opening of the career of Jesus. As the Greek poet Simonides has said: "*It is hard to show oneself a good man*"; and this remarkable narrative reveals to us that the same difficulty which besets all men had to be surmounted by Jesus. It was not without a struggle—a process of temptation and the resisting of temptation—that He finally chose the good and refused the less good.

But observe the character of that Tempta-

tion. The motives which had some power over
His mind were not such as appeal to a vulgar
or an uneducated and slow nature : they were
of the higher type, likely to fascinate a noble,
generous, ardent intellect, which had thought
deeply and aimed high, a mind of the really
educated type.

It was the sense of power, the aspiration to
do something great and to achieve some remarkable exhibition of moral or intellectual
ascendency, that the Tempter appealed to.
Even the mere physical craving for food after
a long fast was presented before the mind
of Jesus as an opportunity of exercising His
power over nature.

In the Temptation *the devil taketh Him
unto an exceeding high mountain and sheweth
Him all the kingdoms of the world and the
glory of them.* Only the dullest and most
witless of critics will make the objection that
it is impossible to see all the kingdoms of the
world from any mountain. The man whose
temptation came in this form was one to whom

the wide prospect of a great stretch of country
was inspiring and creative, revealing far more
than the eye beholds, lifting the mind on the
wings of imagination to a far-reaching outlook
over history and time, and suggesting a vision
of the authority and glory of a world-wide
empire.

In the whole narrative, as most readers
probably will agree, the detail which most
clearly partakes of the nature of parable is the
promise which the Tempter held out on the
summit of the mountain : " *All these things
will I give Thee, if Thou wilt fall down and
worship me* ". The career of ambition and
worldly power is metaphorically expressed as
the worship of Satan ; but to the disciples,
ignorant and simple as they were, that career
had to be presented in a flash of description
and condemnation, such as would cut its way
into their minds.

The man who was tempted by those sug-
gestions and methods was one who had
thought much. He had surveyed in imagina-

tion all the kingdoms of the world ; and the
view of the mighty opportunities open to surpassing intellect and high aims had occupied
His mind and exercised a certain fascination
over it.   To that fascination the Tempter
appealed ; and Jesus deliberately and finally
chose a spiritual kingdom and the power of
truth.   He had considered the world and its
facts ; and He had estimated all things at their
true and eternal value.

How then had He gained this wide outlook
over the kingdoms of the world ?   The more
one knows of the dull, narrow, insensate nature
of the Oriental peasant, the more must one
wonder at the breadth and ardour of mind
that is revealed in the Temptation, and the
more eagerly must one try to imagine the
influences which had educated that unique
personality.

As one reads the biography of Jesus, one
cannot fail to be struck with the effect that
seems to have been exercised on His mind
and nature by the wide prospect from a

lofty elevation. Try to cut out the mountain scenes from His life. How much
poorer would the Gospels be.

It was on a mountain at dawn of day that
He chose from among His disciples twelve,
whom also He named Apostles, "*that He
might send them forth to preach and to have
authority*".

When He was in Jerusalem, His life was
divided between the Mount of Olives and
the Temple. The Temple was the focus of
Hebrew life and religious feeling : the
Mount of Olives was the one point close to
Jerusalem where He could find a wide prospect and a quiet moment to enjoy the
recuperative influences of nature. Every
day He was teaching in the Temple, but
after the day's work He always retired to
the Mount. When on His last journey
He approached Jerusalem from the east,
and came in sight of it, as He crossed the
shoulder of the Mount, the sudden prospect
of that marvellous view over the city drew

from Him His lamentation over the terrible fate that should soon befall it.

His most characteristic discourse was the sermon on another mountain, beside the Sea of Galilee.

The Transfiguration took place on a mountain summit.

It was on a mountain in Galilee that the final instructions were given to the Apostles to *go into all the world, and make disciples of all the nations.*

And similarly, in the present case, the climax of His temptation lay in the vision of worldly power that was suggested by the view from "an exceeding high mountain". The climax is spoiled in the order of Luke's narrative, in which this temptation is put second in order of the three ; and we must beyond a doubt prefer the order of the temptations as Matthew describes them.

In the career of Christ the last scene is a suitable balance to the first. The crisis of the first turned on the survey of worldly

power and glory from a mountain top. The
climax of the last is the mission of the Apostles
from the Galilean mountain to enter into
possession of the whole world. In the cor-
respondence of the two scenes there is that
perfect propriety which characterises the
whole of the biography of Jesus : the ar-
rangement, so entirely natural and unstudied,
has the perfection of consummate art.

Passages like these press on us the idea
that a notable side to the character of Jesus
lay in His poetic and imaginative susceptibility
to the influences of natural scenery. This
susceptibility did not take the form merely of
a liking for the picturesque, which seems to
be rather a fashionable idol of the modern
mind than a deep-seated craving of the human
spirit. It was the suggestiveness of a wide
prospect, the stimulation of the mind accom-
panying the outlook from a point of vantage,
which moved the nature of Jesus, and was
probably a strong influence in determining
His education.

"The Transfiguration took place on a mountain summit."

Surely there is no one among us who has grown up without experiencing the apparent quickening of the pulse, the stronger beating of the heart, the exaltation to a higher plane of feeling, that affect one as he looks over some of the striking prospects in our own land, where historical associations and natural beauty unite to quicken one's patriotism and ennoble one's nature.

That experience in all of us I presume as a point to start from.

I shall not recite an essay on schools and educational methods in ancient Palestine. Information on those subjects is accessible in the biblical encyclopædias and the histories of that period. A man's education lies not in what is common to all, but in what is special to himself. It lies in the use which he resolves to make of the opportunities which the law of his nation or the custom of society or the generosity of some benefactor opens to him.

When sometimes a day-dream or a vision

seems to offer a momentary glimpse into the education of Christ, one thinks of Him on a lofty eminence.   Such a dream I will venture to relate to you.

CHAPTER II

AT NAZARETH

CHAPTER II.

AT NAZARETH.

NEARLY four years ago the governing body of this University permitted me to take advantage of the only opportunity that has ever come to me of seeing the chief places in which the life of Jesus was spent. Without that experience I do not think that any one is equipped to speak or write about ancient history to the highest height of his own powers, such as they are.

I spent a long Sunday afternoon at the village of Nain in the company of one friend, who was sympathetic and responsive to the influences of nature. We ascended the steep slope of Mount Moreh, on the skirts of which the village stands, and beheld the wide prospect over the plain of Esdraelon or

(45)

Megiddo, that great valley which runs right across Palestine from the Mediterranean Sea on the west to the River Jordan eight hundred feet below sea-level on the east, dividing that mountainous land as by a deep trench or chasm, on the north of which is the hill-country of Galilee, and on the south are the hills of Samaria rising still further south to Mount Ephraim and the highlands of Judah.

We read the touching story of the Widow's son, the story which has made Nain familiar to every educated person so long as the world shall last. We looked out over that great plain of Megiddo, which lay outstretched before us, to Mount Tabor a few miles north, and to Mount Carmel far away to the west, and between them we looked towards Nazareth, from which we had just come, and we could catch a glimpse of its highest-lying buildings over the intervening hills on the northern edge of the great plain.

Then we read the brilliant pages in which Professor George Adam Smith has described that plain of Megiddo ; and there came to me the thoughts which I shall try to express to you in words too halting and insufficient— words in which some ideas are caught from the eloquent paragraphs of the book which we had just been reading.

Nazareth lies deep in a rounded hollow among the hills of southern Galilee. Its houses cluster in the depths of the hollow around the Fountain of the Virgin, or climb in straggling, haphazard order up the hillsides. The day before, coming from the Sea of Galilee by way of Cana, we had looked down from the northern edge into the cup where Nazareth lay, in its isolation and seclusion, quiet and restful, apparently cut off entirely from the world, " *alike unknowing and unknown* ".

That first impression had been intensified when we went down into the hollow and looked up to the encompassing hills, a narrow, unbroken circle, like a barrier defending Nazareth from the world, seeming to repress the tendency to wander or to travel, and to throw the inhabitants back on their own company and their own thoughts. One felt that, in a child who was naturally inclined towards meditation, this inclination would inevitably be strengthened and confirmed, as he grew up in Nazareth. But one also felt that the surroundings seemed too narrow, and there was a danger lest, in that little hollow amid the rather featureless and monotonous succession of bare hills through which we had come to Nazareth, the sympathetic and responsive mind of such a child as we have thought about might be cramped and hardened and starved from want of suggestion in the scenes around him. The satirical question of the Jews, whether any good thing could come out of Nazareth, began to assume a new meaning in our minds. It did not seem easy to understand how history had given an affirmative answer to that question.

But when, a few hours later, we proceeded on our journey southwards, we quickly realised that our first impression of Nazareth had been incomplete and misleading. We crossed the summit of the hills that shut in the little town on the south ; and immediately what a scene lay before us. Before us lay the great plain of Megiddo, and opposite us from the southern edge of the plain rose the mountain-land of central Palestine. Away to the right we saw Mount Carmel, closing the valley on the west and dividing it from the plain of Sharon. On the left the eastern view was closed and the plain was narrowed by Mount Tabor, Mount Moreh (round whose slopes lay Nain, Endor, Shunem and Jezreel) and Mount Gilboa. Nowhere, not even from the summit of the Mount of Olives, with Jerusalem before and the Dead Sea behind, has the historian or the philosophic thinker a more inspiring and impressive view than that from the brow south of Nazareth.

To the young Jewish boy of that ancient time every corner of the great valley, every rising ground of the surrounding hills, was filled with memories of a mighty past and the lessons in patriotism and religion that they conveyed, filled too with stirring and impressive sights of the present, and suggesting visions of the future.

And so the young Jew of Nazareth looks over the valley towards the hills which contain and conceal Samaria and Jerusalem, Bethel and Bethlehem, with the eyes of intelligence and sympathy and fascination. Every name and every scene is full of meaning to him. The past history of his people lives before him as he looks around.

On Mount Carmel Elijah is pitted as a solitary champion against the four hundred and fifty prophets of Baal; and with him is God, and victory.

Over there in the front of the Samarian hills is Hadadrimmon in the valley of Megiddo, where the mourning has become a proverb in Israel, since Josiah for once disregarded the message of God, and was defeated and slain at the first charge of the Egyptian army.

To the east, on Mount Tabor, Deborah the prophetess from the south meets Barak with his warriors of the north, and before them far and wide extends the large Canaanite host which holds all the great plain ; and the men of the hill-tribes, resolute to maintain the national religion, cut through the centre of the enemy, while the stars in their courses fight against Sisera, the storm makes the great plain into a marsh where their chariots of iron only impede and disorder the Canaanite ranks, and the Kishon swollen high with rain sweeps them away in its torrent waters.

Further to the east, between Mount Tabor and Mount Moreh, is Endor, where King Saul played a game against the powers of the world of death, in violation of the law that he had himself enacted, staking his honour and his religion and his kingdom and his life, and losing everything. And there, a few miles further south, divided from the narrow ridge of Mount Moreh by the deep and narrow Vale of Jezreel, is Mount Gilboa, where the last scene is being played : on the mountain is arrayed the whole host of Israel, while below them in the Vale of Jezreel are the victorious Philistines, out of sight at first but emerging as they win their way round and up the mountain.   The advantage in position, in experience of generalship, and in personal bravery, is lost by the king who had ceased to trust himself or to be true to his religion.

Almost in the same place the Three Hundred, with the sword of the Lord and of Gideon, drive before them the invading host of the Midianites in midnight panic.

There lies Jezreel, the scene of so much of Israel's glory and crime.   There is the vineyard of Naboth.   Behind it the Vale of Jezreel runs away down to the Jordan ; at its foot, far down behind Mount Moreh—not in sight from this point, but a longer excursion towards Jezreel has made you able to call it up in memory—the grim fortress of Bethshan rises in the distance *like a ship at sea*, and the heads

of Saul and Jonathan are fastened on its walls.
Up that sloping Vale the rebel Jehu has driven
furiously, and he comes into view at the summit beside Jezreel. You know him by the
pace that he drives at, and you know the fate
which awaits the royal family that led the
kingdom astray.

That valley of Megiddo, a great cleft across
the country, was the natural road from the
coast to the east ; and there the never-ending
battle between light and darkness, between
good and evil, was still being fought, as it
had been in the past, and would be in the
future. The barbarism of primitive savagery
invaded the land with the Bedouin tribes of
the east. The barbarism of too precocious
civilisation, with its reckless pursuit of pleasure
and money and power, came up from the sea
with the Phœnicians and the Romans.

The boy watched the Roman travellers, merchants, messengers, soldiers, officials, going east
and returning west ; he heard much about the
glory and power of the great Empire, the

oppressor of the Hebrews, which kept its garrison even in the Holy City, and made the high priests of Jerusalem its slaves. Nazareth was to him like a hermitage beside a great centre of life : he could pass in a few moments from the quiet seclusion of his home into full view of the busy world, and then retire again to peace.

And, as the past had been, so the future would be. The valley of Megiddo, as any thoughtful mind could foresee, would hereafter be the scene of as great battles as had ever been fought there.

The event has already justified the antici-pation. Mohammedanism there waged the decisive wars against Christianity—battles more decisive than the capture of Jerusalem itself—whether against the defenders of the Byzantine faith and government, or against the invasion of the crusaders from the west. Napoleon won a victory in the valley under Mount Tabor, just where Deborah and Barak had fought ; but his victory was the last

"The boy watched the Roman travellers, merchants, messengers, soldiers, officials, going east and returning west."

effort of human genius fighting against impossible conditions, and was almost immediately followed by retreat.

And then—last scene of all—when the *"unclean spirits of evil go forth unto the kings of the world to gather them together unto the war of the great day,"* where else could the Jewish child foresee that the battle must be fought except in that plain? And so, in the vision in the Isle of Patmos, many years later, one of the disciples of that Child looked upon the preparations for that great battle, and he saw that "the kings of the whole world had gathered them together into the place which is called in Hebrew Ar-Megiddo". Would that detail ever have taken the exact form in which it is set down in the Revelation, if the childhood of Jesus had not been nourished on the study of history as it was revealed to Him in the view from the brow of the hill at Nazareth?

One cannot but ask whether we may here recognise in the Apocalypse the echo of one of the lessons, not otherwise recorded, in which Jesus educated His disciples by parable and apologue, in history and in insight, so that, immediately after His death, the highest and best-trained intellects in the nation " *marvelled* " at their words, and " *took knowledge of them that they had been with Jesus* " ?

Either that : or else the minds of all the Hebrews had become so familiar with the historic importance of Megiddo, that any of their prophets who looked into the future would naturally see in that valley the theatre of the great battle of the nations.

Most impressive of all to the young Jew of Nazareth was the fact that he should be standing there, and not in his own family home in the distant land of Judah at Bethlehem. Israel had deserted God, and the issue had been that the Galilean hills and the great plain of Megiddo had passed from them ; and for a time there was not a Hebrew in Galilee of the Gentiles. Then the southern Jews, who had remained true to their religion, began to settle in that

pleasant northern land, which had once be-
longed to the lost tribes.

But those emigrants from the south, who had
made their new home in the pleasant land of
the north, still clung to their connection with
Jerusalem, because their meeting at that centre
of their religion was the guarantee of their
national unity and permanence. They made
regular visits to Jerusalem ; and thus they kept
alive their national feeling and their hold on
their religion. They also kept fresh and
living the memory of their ancient home and
their tribal and family connection in Southern
Palestine. Nazareth was merely their place
of residence, though the outer world fancied
that it was their city and fatherland ; but
they knew in their own hearts as a fragrant
memory that their own city and true home
was far away in the highlands of the south.
An idea, which lay hidden deep in their minds
and was hardly known outside the household
circle, was a stronger force in their nature
than all the tender associations of childhood

and lifelong residence. And that in itself was an education to the child in the Nazarene house. He learned from infancy to estimate the ideal above the actual, to regard immediate material surroundings as temporary and evanescent, and to look for truth and reality in the world of thought.

Living among such scenes and in such circumstances, the thoughtful Jew of Nazareth could not fail to learn thoroughly the lesson, so that it became part of his mind and nature, that religion makes the nation, and the loss of religion must destroy it.

But that lesson is not enough by itself alone to make an education. What is the religion that is to make the nation? What is the essential and permanent factor, what is the creative and vitalising element, in religion? Will the traditional worship in its Judean centre be sufficient for Israel?

The lessons had to be carried further, and the experience of Nazareth alone was not sufficient.

CHAPTER III

A HEBREW BOY'S EDUCATION

CHAPTER III.

A HEBREW BOY'S EDUCATION.

THE scenes of nature and the localities in which great events have occurred have a meaning only to the educated mind ; they carry no significance and no teaching for the savage, the ignorant, or the narrow mind. One may ask how far was that young Jew of Nazareth trained to appreciate the inspiration of that wonderful scene, which was always open to him within half an hour's walk from his own door?

About the answer to that question we cannot hesitate.

No education was ever so well adapted to train a thoughtful child in the appreciation of his own country, to render its past history living and real to him, to strengthen his patriotic feeling, to make every geographical name and scene full of meaning and historic truth, as the training which every Hebrew child then received. He learned to know one small collection of books thoroughly, and that library gave him a training in literature and in history, in philosophic insight and in religious feeling.

I doubt if modern scholars sufficiently appreciate the Hebrew education in that period. They are never weary of describing the narrowness, the ignorance, the prejudice and the sordid formalism of those old Jews. It is true that those old Hebrews were ignorant of much that we know. But there is no fallacy so universal, and none so dangerous in this world, as the opinion that the man who does not know exactly what we ourselves know is an uneducated and ignorant person. The man who really knows is the man who has discovered truth for himself, and not the man who has been taught results.

If most of the Jews of that time knew nothing about Homer and Æschylus, all of them were familiar with the great poets and prophets and law-givers of their own land. They had none of the scientific interest and aptitude of the Greeks, and the inventions of Archimedes were strange and incomprehensible to them; but no one would now maintain that an educated man must necessarily understand the latest scientific theories and inventions of the age. We all know that the modern Board-school child can expose the errors and show up the ignorance of the great Greek astronomers and investigators; and, beyond a doubt, children a century hence will marvel at the ignorance of the great physicists and electricians of our day. Children will marvel, because they have only been taught results; but educated men will admire the great discoverers whether of the Greek period or of our own day. They discovered, and therefore they knew, in their own line and their own degree; yet the greatest of them made only a

small advance in the long road towards knowledge.

And, further, the educated man has learned
that many roads towards many goals of
knowledge stretch out before us, and that he
who has struggled forward a little distance
on any of them has done well, and may take
rank among the men who know.   If the Jews
were far behind some of the Greeks in some of
the paths of intellectual and artistic attainment,
they were far beyond them in the even more
important paths of moral progress and of
national education.

The lofty pride with which the Jew then
looked down on the Gentile was not merely
the result of ignorant bigotry : its strength lay
in this, that the Jew stood both morally and
intellectually on a far higher level than the
Gentile.   Most of us know by experience the
feeling with which the men who have been
accustomed to play the game fairly look
down on those who are incapable of obeying
the laws of the game and would snatch at

unfair advantages.   To play the fair game
is not the whole of morality : but " *'tis
something, nay, 'tis much* ".   So the Jews
were not perfect masters of a wide and true
morality ; but at least they stood on an
immensely higher level than that of pagan
society.

The Hebrew conception of a general
national system of education was pitched
on the same superior level.

It is true that the most admirable side of
the Greek city constitution lay in the firm
grasp of the principle that it is the duty
of the State to educate its citizens ; but the
education which the cities provided was
narrow in its conception, shallow and unreal
in its character, and destitute of any vivifying
and invigorating ideal.

As for the Roman imperial system, its one
educational aim seems to have been to prevent
the mass of the people from thinking too
much, and to provide them with abundant
and cheap amusements.

The result was that the Græco-Roman world was decaying and dying from the dearth of true educational ideals.

Only among the Hebrews was there any real, salutary, invigorating system of national education.   Only among them was the principle firmly grasped and boldly enunciated, that the poor man's son has as much right to be educated up to his true capacity as the rich man's son, and that both alike should be taught to work.

We are most of us so busy studying, as patient and unquestioning disciples, the very latest German authority—not necessarily the greatest, but we must have the latest—who has printed or lectured on the New Testament, that we have no time to act on the rule of the great Germans and search after truth for ourselves, regardless of authority.   We only see what the teachers whom we worship have said. But the truth is this, and it is a truth which, will soon be discovered and emphasised by the

Germans, and will then be brought over and accepted among us, that the Hebrew nation was at that time the most highly educated people in the world—in the true meaning of the word education.

CHAPTER IV

AT JERUSALEM

CHAPTER IV.

AT JERUSALEM.

THE surroundings of Nazareth alone did not furnish a broad enough education ; but that young scholar, whom we are imagining, saw more than the land of the north. He went up to Jerusalem among the southern mountains every year, and saw his own land among his own people. He saw, also, what the Jewish system had made of the land and the nation.

Nearly two hundred years ago the Jews had freed themselves from foreign rule. A small people in a little country, untrained to war, they had, by sheer belief in their God and the strength thereof, defeated army after army of a great military power, and won by the sword freedom for their own religion and their own customs. They had kept their religion and they had excluded the foreigner ; and the result had been failure. Their own city under their own rule always *killed the prophets and stoned them that were sent unto her.* Their religion had not been sufficient for them. It was killing the national heart and fossilising the national life.

The foreigner could not be kept out. A wider idea of unity had been introduced into the world, and was being slowly, blindly, irrationally, unintelligently wrought out amid bloodshed and cruelty by the destroying and yet consolidating Empire of Rome. The brotherhood of the nations was an idea too noble and too wide for the old Jewish religion ; but the idea had come into the world and it could not be cast out. The old Judaism must be enlarged to contain the new idea ; but that old religion seemed to have lost the power of growth, and to have become a rigid, cast-iron system, which rejected and abhorred the thought of growing.

This, then, was the further lesson that had to be learned. The nation and the world needed a religion of growth, of development, of evolution.

That the contemplation of the scene, as one looks over Jerusalem, suggested such thoughts in the mind of Jesus from childhood upwards —thoughts that grew more clear and definite as the years rolled on—seems not open to doubt.

The statements in the Third Gospel that, during the final visit to Jerusalem, He used to retire to the Mount of Olives every evening (xxi. 37), and that this was a custom with Him (xxii. 39), might fairly be understood as true also of previous visits to the city.

This inference is confirmed by the Fourth Gospel : St. John expressly mentions that on an earlier visit to Jerusalem, at evening *Jesus went to the Mount of Olives, and early in the morning He came again into the Temple.*

Still earlier in His life an example of His already formed habit of going forth in the evening from the city to the Mount may, in all probability, be found in the story of Nicodemus, who *came unto Him by night.* On that elevated place how naturally the illustration suggested itself to Him, and how vividly it would come home to the mind of Nicodemus : *The wind bloweth where it listeth, and thou hearest the voice thereof, but knowest not whence it cometh, and whither it goeth.* In a northern land we, who spend our life mainly within the walls of houses, often fail to appreciate the peculiar tone given to the everyday life and thought of those nations whom we study so much, Greeks, Romans and Jews, by the fact that they lived in the open air. Among all the modern books which offer an ideal picture of the life of the Mediterranean peoples, modern or ancient, I know only one in which blows the breath of the open air ; and yet, unless you catch that spirit, you are divided by a wall from the life of Greek or Jew, and can never understand it with true sympathy.

"He used to retire to the Mount of Olives every evening."

But, as you read the words which St. John has preserved, you feel yourself out on the quiet hillside, with the breath of the evening moving gently around you ; and you remember that the time was the season of the year about the Passover, when, in the poet's words,

Spring's awakening breath will woo the earth
To feed with kindliest dew its favourite flower.

You remember also that the same poet thinks about

Evening's breath, wandering here and there ;

and you begin to ask whether the earlier printed text is not correct (though now discarded by editors) in those other lines of his :—

The breath of the moist air is light
Around its unexpanded buds.

The very word is the same, for the Greek word means "the breath" as well as "the wind" ; and the literal rendering of Jesus' saying is "*The breath (of the air) breatheth where it will*". And then you know that Nicodemus, desirous to speak secretly with

Jesus, did not need to slink with veiled head into a garret or a cellar where the poor Galilean peasant lodged ; but, knowing His custom, went forth to the Mount.

And, if it be asked why it was His habit to spend the evenings on the Mount, there is only one answer : " *Come, and ye shall see* ". No one who looks over that wonderful prospect is likely to doubt that its ethical and historical interest—and in the Jewish mind the ethical and the historical aspects were identified—was always present to Him there, and formed the attraction to draw Him thither.

We have only to read over the various incidents in the life of Jesus which occurred on the Mount of Olives, in order to see how suggestive the prospect was to Him, and how naturally on that commanding height His mind turned to anticipate the future fate of the city over which he was looking, and to review the circumstances of the coming judgment of the whole world, comparing them with the great judgment in past history, the Flood. It was on the Mount, in view of the sea which flowed over the cities of the Plain, that His most grave and impressive discourse on watchfulness and responsibility and readiness to meet the sure and sudden judgment was delivered.

Equally certain is it that the scenes, through which the annual journeys to and from Jerusalem led Him, were not without effect on His mind.

More clearly and insistently than in any other land, the philosophy of history, the Will of God as it has wrought in the world, is written on the landscape of Palestine; and the rightly educated mind cannot but read it. And yet there are strange examples of blindness to the surpassing interest which that country has for the historian.

It is, indeed, easy to understand why the large class of tourists to whom Switzerland represents the ideal of natural beauty must be disappointed with Palestine.

The scenery, more especially in the central and southern regions, is rarely in itself grand or picturesque or impressive in the ordinary sense ; and it is in an equal degree devoid of the rich beauty of high cultivation and productiveness.   The hills as a rule are bald, bare and featureless.   The terraces by which in happier times the soil was supported on the slopes have almost everywhere been destroyed, and the soil has been washed down into the hollows, where it impedes the outflow of the waters and produces marshes.   Thus the land is desolate and unattractive.   In general the slopes and hillsides are a wilderness of stones and rocks, where a few scanty shrubs can barely find a hold, and the glens a wilderness of marsh, with a scanty rim of cultivable land above the level of the bog and below the level of the bare rocks, just sufficient to grow food for the miserable and scanty population.

Those who would enjoy the scenery of Palestine must bring a trained mind, familiar with its history, able to perceive the unity and the purpose in the evolution of that history, able to understand and sympathise with all that the country meant to its own people. They must have learnt the lesson that in every case the country has much to do with the formation of its people's character, that in Palestine especially the country was the decisive factor in making the people, and that the desolation of the land is a necessary part of the history of its people.

There are, however, great and justly respected scholars, whose want of sympathy is, at first sight, astonishing and disappointing.

It would be not altogether a useless or unfair test to classify the interpreters of Hebrew history according to their power of comprehending the nature of the country and of reading in its features the history of the people. Take, for example, what Renan says about the view of Jerusalem and its influence on the mind of Jesus.

The parched appearance of Nature in the

neighbourhood of Jerusalem must have added to the dislike Jesus had for the place. The valleys are without water; the soil arid and stony. Looking into the valley of the Dead Sea, the view is somewhat striking; elsewhere it is monotonous. The hill of Mizpeh, around which cluster the most ancient historical remembrances of Israel, alone relieves the eye.

The allusion which Renan makes to the Dead Sea shows that in this passage he has in mind the view from the summit of the Mount of Olives. The brief description of Mizpeh, quite in the most approved guide-book style, is the sole historical thought that occurs to him. The least educated of Cook's tourists could hardly have seen less in that scene than the distinguished and eloquent French scholar. And yet Renan was a Breton, one of a race in whom we should have expected that the sensibility to the unseen and spiritual side of the world would be highly developed.

But the fact is that he came to the scene

with his mind made up and his eyes closed
to a great part of the character and work of
Jesus. He could not possibly understand the
emotions and ideas which that marvellous prospect, the most entrancing in the world to the
true and open-minded student of history—the
view over Jerusalem to the hills of Bethlehem
and to Mizpeh—over the Dead Sea and the
Jordan to the land of Moab and Ammon and
the country of Gilead, rising like a great
mountain-wall in the east—must rouse in
the mind of Jesus ; because, if he began to
understand it, his sentimental and narrow
conception of Jesus would no longer have been
possible. As long as he could not forget his
prepossessions nor widen his views, the scene
necessarily remained to him a mere arid, un-
suggestive and repellent desert. The Jesus
whom Renan pictured to himself and set before
his readers had a positive dislike for that *city
of pedantry, acrimony, quarrels and littleness of
mind*, set in its parched and dreary landscape ;
but the Jesus of history and reality could not

look at it or think of it without an outbreak of love and despair: " *How often would I have gathered thy children together even as a hen gathereth her chickens under her wings, and ye would not*".

CHAPTER V

THE DIVINE IN THE WORLD

CHAPTER V.

THE DIVINE IN THE WORLD.

IF you ask how I know that the Child of Nazareth drew such inspiration and such lessons from the scenes in view of which He grew up to manhood, the answer is that the truth of Christ is the lesson of the world's history. It is misleading and unreal to say that Christianity is true because Christ declared it : the right way of putting it is that Christ declared His message because He knew that it was true. You have only to look into the past with the understanding eye, and you see there Christianity written in large letters : either you do not understand, or you read there the message of the Christ. The history of the world previously is the preparation for Him : subsequent history proceeds from Him.

(85)

One must feel a profound pity for the man who cannot see this truth in history : all is to him so dark and perplexing, whereas to the eye which looks rightly all things stand out so clear and simple.

In that country you cannot but learn, and every leading spirit among the Jews always learned and proclaimed, the one great principle of history : the story of the world is simply the gradual unfolding of the Will of God within those conditions of time and space that hedge us in.   It is the same principle that modern science teaches and flatters itself to have dis-covered—the principle that there is unity in Nature, that the order of Nature is uniform, universal, inexorable.   Reality or truth is power, and power is God ; or, as St. Paul puts it, *the Kingdom of God is not in word, but in power:* truth lies not in abstract theory but in actual concrete effectiveness.   To test whether an idea is true, whether if it is of God, watch it in its effects : if it lives and grows, it is true and Divine.

And so, to understand the present, we look back into the past. In the gradual evolution of history we see the gradual revelation, step by step, of the Will of God. Now that revelation must culminate at the due season, or, to use again the word of St. Paul, "*in the fulness of time*". It must culminate; it must reach the fully developed stage at the proper moment. That is inexorably necessary: it lies in the nature of the case : it is involved in the very meaning of the word evolution. And this is that culminating stage in the evolution of the Will of God at the due season. When the world is ready for it, the perfect revelation must come, and that perfect revelation is the Divine Will, the Divine Nature, in such form as to be intelligible to man and to remain among men. As the Jews put it, the Christos, the Messiah, must come : as St. John expresses it, the Truth must *become flesh and dwell among us.*

And further, this Christ, this Truth made flesh, must die, because in this world the idea is not real, unless it so seizes and possesses the bearer that he gives his life up to it, and spends his life for it. What great truth has ever become effective and real among men, unless it has found a soul ready to die for it? That is the law; you can see it in the days of Socrates and in all time.

Yet not only must this Christ die; He must also live. To be real He must be effective and permanent.

A dead Christ, such as Matthew Arnold sets before us in that sketch of the philosophy of history which he puts into the mouth of the Swiss recluse Obermann :—

> Now he is dead! Far hence he lies
>   In the lorn Syrian town,
> And on his grave, with shining eyes,
>   The Syrian stars look down—

such a dead Christ would be useless to the world. If those exquisitely pathetic lines expressed the truth, the hopeless conclusion of the stanzas in which the poet continues must also be accepted :—

In vain men still, with hoping new,
  Regard his death-place dumb,
And say the stone is not yet to,
  And wait for words to come.

Ah, from that silent sacred land,
  Of sun, and arid stone,
And crumbling wall, and sultry sand,
  Comes now one word alone!

From David's lips this word did roll,
  'Tis true and living yet:
No man can save his brother's soul,
  Nor pay his brother's debt.

Every man must work out his own salvation for himself and by himself.   No man can pay another's debt.

> Thou hast been, shalt be, art, alone.

And yet there is an exception, as the poet himself immediately goes on to admit. Though man is separated from other men, the finite being parted from the finite, yet he is not wholly cut off from the Divine and the infinite. That connection is never severed.   And so the poet has to correct himself, as that thought—

though in a narrow and poorer form—occurs
to his mind ; and he continues :—

> Or, if not quite alone, yet they
> Which touch thee are unmating things—
> Ocean and clouds and night and day,
> Lorn autumns and triumphant springs,
> And life, and others' joy and pain,
> And love, if love, of happier men.

Such is the disappointing and chilling summary
of all that the poet can perceive of Divine and
eternal in the world in which men live.   But
a dead Christ would be no more than a man ;
and all other men would be separated absolutely
from him.   Only a living Christ could be
Divine, and so connected with and related to
every human being.

One cannot but observe in those words,
in which Matthew Arnold describes the landscape of Palestine, the note which he has
probably caught from Renan.   The strain of
sentimentalism and unreality must always
produce a certain blindness to the deepest
characteristics of *that silent sacred land*, and

prevent one from seeing there ought save desolation and aridity and ruin.

The necessity that the Christ must always be living governs the expression of the Gospels. The saying occurs repeatedly : *The Son of Man must suffer, and be killed*, but always the completing words are added immediately, *and rise again*. The half truth in this case would be no truth.

And so the Truth, as expressed by St. Paul, as lived by Christ, unites in itself both death and life : the Crucifixion and the Resurrection are two aspects of one fact, and neither is intelligible or complete without the other.

That Truth, as it stands revealed to us within the conditions of space and time, is the life of Jesus. That is the one most real, most true fact amid the never-ceasing flux and change, in which the world's history expresses itself. In comparison with that, all else is unreal, delusive, mere empty opinion (as Plato would call it) and not real knowledge. The life of Jesus is the reality on which the life of all men rests. Christ died, and yet He lives. The Crucifixion and the Resurrection are two sides of the one truth, each by itself incomplete, each requiring the other to explain and justify it.

"The Crucifixion and the Resurrection are two aspects
of one fact."

CHAPTER VI

SUPERHUMAN NOT SUPERNATURAL

CHAPTER VI.

SUPERHUMAN NOT SUPERNATURAL.

NOW there are many persons who are ready and eager to maintain as a matter of purely philosophical speculation that there must necessarily be a connection and a relationship of man to God, of the world to the power from whom and through whom it derives and maintains its existence. They champion that view as a matter of abstract theory, and they are ready to talk about it, to reason about it, to assume it as a premise in their arguments ; but they are not ready to admit it in concrete fact and living reality. It remains to them true in word, but not in power.

No such connection of God with man, however, can be real, unless it so expresses itself as to become a power among men and touch

the minds of men in general.   It must manifest itself in a form that can be understood of
men, a form that can be powerful and living
among men ; otherwise it remains apart and
powerless and unreal, a theoretic and abstract
subject of contemplation and speculation
among the few, not a truth that lives in the
world of humanity.   That is something of
what St. John meant when he said that the
Word became flesh and dwelt among us.   The
Divine nature did not simply remain apart
from mankind, but expressed and embodied
itself in such form as men could comprehend,
and came among them.

The reason why so many persons are un-
willing to admit the full consequences of their
philosophic theory lies in this.   Any such
manifestation of the Divine presence in the
world in real, actual, living form must necessarily involve some element of the superhuman.
It would be a self-contradiction to say that
the Divine presence in the world can embody
and express itself in purely and simply human

form : it must be human to be known of men; but it must be superhuman to be useful to men, to be and remain itself.

But, in their eagerness to attain a seeming but false simplicity, many would deny the existence and even the possibility of the super-human element in the actual world. They label that idea with the incorrect and question-begging term of " miraculous " or " super-natural," and point the finger of scorn and ridicule at those who " believe in miracles and the supernatural ". They restrict the term " natural " to the sum of ordinary human experience and acquired knowledge ; and the vast unknown that lies beyond, outside human ken, they set aside and ignore. But they either forget, or they have entirely failed to understand, that, in so far as in theory they have spoken about the Divine action in history, they have thereby admitted the existence of the superhuman in the world. It is really a proof of ignorance and narrow-ness, not of knowledge and broad-mindedness, that they can put out of their reckoning the vast ocean which still remains beyond the present sweep of human faculties, but which may not always remain so, for the growth of education and science has made us distinctly more conscious of and sensitive to its existence than we were a generation ago. Every one who has lived through that period must feel that this growing consciousness of the reality of the as yet uncomprehended region in nature is one of the most remarkable features in the development of recent thought.

It is therefore unfair and irrational to confound the "superhuman" with the "supernatural". The "natural" includes both the human and the superhuman.

And the term "miraculous" is too vague and question-begging. In so far as it connotes "supernatural," it is a term that should be very carefully and sparingly employed; but in so far as it means only "superhuman," it is unnecessary and misleading, since it conveys a false innuendo. The word belongs to an early and undeveloped stage of thought, when men could hardly accept any idea or thought or principle of a general kind as true, unless it seemed to them to be guaranteed by marvellous or miraculous accompaniments. They craved the marvellous, in order to help them to trust what was beyond their comprehension; and they found it or invented it. But, as the power of thinking develops, men learn that the marvellous or miraculous lies in the sphere of the inconceivable and the unintelligible, and that it belongs to ignorance, not to knowledge. The word has lost its meaning for them, and they distrust anything that has become associated with it. The strange and marvellous accompaniments, in which a primitive age found confirmation of truth, seem to a modern mind to cast doubt upon truth. For the moment those accompaniments should be, not ridiculed, but set on one side as uncomprehended : in due course, as knowledge grows, they will find their place in a new conception and a broader science.

It is a grand yet a common blunder to lay exaggerated stress on those sensuous accompaniments, and to fancy that we can really place ourselves at the point of view of those who become sensitive to Divine truth only through them.   It is as stupid and irrational an error to refuse the truth because of those sensuous encumbrances, as it is to insist that the truth cannot be accepted without them. They are rather a branch of human history than of Divine reality, an evanescent and not a permanent factor in the growth of Divine knowledge.   They have their reality and their value, to be estimated by the effect they have produced on human history ; but their value should not be exaggerated, any more than it should be slighted.

It is impossible for us in the present day to understand perfectly and sympathise fully with the thoughts of a remote past and a primitive, uneducated, undeveloped way of contemplating the world.   Especially, those who live amid the surroundings of universities, and are mainly occupied with the attempt to comprehend the more advanced forms and subjects of thought, are apt to lose the sense for the real character of primitive religion. But this at least must be kept in mind : the sensuous and material incidents which accompany the perception of the Divine nature by man, that is to say, the manifestation of the Divine nature to man— such incidents as are alluded to in the Prologue—are accidental, not essential : they are marks of weakness in the percipient, and proofs of insensibility to higher forms of revelation.

As the author of the Fourth Gospel evidently knew, it was as a concession to the weakness and imperfection of the disciples' nature that they were convinced by sight and touch and hearing ; and he remembers the words: "*Because thou hast seen Me, thou hast believed: blessed are they that have not seen, and yet have believed*". St. Paul had some conception of the development from the sensuous to the non-sensuous perception of truth, when he said: "*Though we have known*

Christ after the flesh, yet now we know Him so no more ". And perhaps some veiled expression of the need for such a development should be read in the experience of Elijah, when he was bidden *go forth and stand upon the mount before the Lord. And, behold, the Lord passed by, and a great and strong wind rent the mountains ; but the Lord was not in the wind : and after the wind an earthquake ; but the Lord was not in the earthquake : and after the earthquake a fire ; but the Lord was not in the fire : and after the fire a sound of gentle stillness.* Was that a sound which affected Elijah's ear—perhaps as if

> there crept
> A little noiseless noise among the leaves—

or did it speak direct to the mind?

The Divine action in the world is not " supernatural," but, in the strictest sense, " natural " ; for it constitutes and gives being and form to nature ; yet it must in the nature of things be and remain superhuman. And so too every revelation and manifestation of

"Blessed are they that have not seen, and yet believed."

the Divine power to man must be in a sense superhuman, inasmuch as it must descend to the plane of the human faculties and become apparent to human senses and powers of acquiring knowledge. It must, though in itself infinite and eternal, unshackled by the conditions of space and time, submit to the fetters of those conditions in order that it may be cognisable by man who lives under them. While it remains upon its own plane, it is indeed always *closer than breathing and nearer than hands and feet.* But, so long as it is restricted to that higher plane, *the ear of man cannot hear, and the eye of man cannot see.* Hence, while on the one hand the revelation of the Divine will to man is a necessary part of the order of nature, and is therefore strictly " natural," it must, on the other hand, necessarily be " superhuman," because it causes and constitutes the gradual elevation of mere human nature towards the Divine nature.

If then we read history as the Hebrew prophets understood it, and as the Jewish education amid the scenes of the Jewish land must fix it in the really thoughtful mind—if we see in the history of man the gradual evolution of the Divine will—then the inevitable conclusion is that the Divine purpose— the Divine as present in the world in that relationship between man and God of which every true poet and every great thinker has had some conception, however dim and unsatisfying his expression of it has sometimes been—must seek completion by manifesting itself in a form intelligible to man ; and this is otherwise expressed by saying that it must become flesh and dwell among men.

But, in so far as the Divine descends to the plane on which man lives, just in so far must its manifestations be partial, local, lasting for a time and then seemingly withdrawn, granted to one human being and withheld from another.   There must be a favoured nation, a favoured land, and favoured individuals, as there can never be equality among men or uniformity in nature.   It is not that any nation or any land is absolutely cut off from the Divine nature, or debarred utterly from coming into communication and communion with it; but men are not equally ready or able to respond to the Divine.

In every communication which takes place between the Divine and the human, there is required not merely the wish of the Divine to reveal itself—for that condition is always fulfilled, and the Divine nature that encompasses us is always pressing itself upon us—there is also required a suitable condition of the will and mind and body of man, able to respond and to become sensitive to the impression. The revelation can never be wholly one-sided. The man who is to hear the Divine message must be attuned in his whole frame to the Divine pulsation; and it is only few men on rare occasions who are so tuned.

In many nations and in all ages there have been individuals who could hear the Divine voice : *because that which may be known of God is manifest in them, for God manifested it unto*

*them: for the invisible nature of the Divine,
viz., His eternal power and Godhead, is clearly
seen ever since the creation of the world, being
perceived through the works of creation.* And
all men *show the work of the Law written in
their hearts, their conscience bearing witness
therewith:* inasmuch as *He left not Himself
without witness.*

But hardly have there been found in any
nation a succession of persons to respond to
the Divine impulse, to hear the Divine voice,
and to be so possessed by the Divine message
as to take the odium of preaching it boldly
and stake their life on the issue. In many
nations we trace the beginning and germs of
true religion. In some we can trace a certain
development and elevation in the national
ideas of religion ; but, as a practical fact, the
religious history of almost all peoples has been,
after a certain time, generally a very brief time,
one of degeneration and degradation, not of
elevation and progress. The many causes
which stifle religious feeling proved too strong

in almost every case : in some cases the fibre
of the race seemed to degenerate amid luxury
and success, in other cases conquest or massacre
destroyed the more vigorous and noble element
in a race, in others a crafty and ambitious
hereditary priesthood distorted religious ideas
to selfish ends ; and so on through all the range
of crime and error.

In the Hebrew nation for many centuries
there had been produced a series of prophets
and seers, who caught the illuminating torch
each from his predecessor. In their hands
through a long succession the Divine message
had grown fuller, clearer and more emphatic.
The great prophets learned the lesson of the
past and added to it themselves. There was a
steady development in insight into the Divine
nature and will, and in the power of applying
that insight to the national requirements. The
nation and its religious conceptions developed,
lagging indeed behind the prophets, always
seeming to the prophets to be slipping back
into idolatry with its inevitable concomitant

immorality : for a low conception of the Divine wishes was always associated with low ideals of life and conduct.

The productive vigour in the nation had seemed to be spent, and the great race of the prophets seemed to be at an end, when John the Baptist appeared to carry on the succession.

His message was a simple one. The series of the prophets had in their message gradually wrought out and given form, though only in vague fashion, to the truth that a more perfect revelation of the Divine nature must in due time come. John recognised that the time had arrived, and that the line of the prophets was now to culminate in the perfect revelation of the purpose and person of God.

CHAPTER VII

THE HISTORICAL JESUS THE ETERNAL CHRIST

CHAPTER VII.

THE HISTORICAL JESUS THE ETERNAL CHRIST.

IN the preceding chapters the identity of the eternal Christ and the historical Jesus has been taken as self-evident, as following directly and inevitably from the belief that the Divine power exists as a real power in the world, concerning itself with human affairs. A Divine power which did not concern itself with humanity would be valueless and non-existent for mankind, the mere abstraction of a philosophic fancy, less real than the Gods of Epicurus. True reason must recognise that the real existence of the Divine power implies a God who takes interest in man, and that such interest must move on to its completion in the manifestation of God to man, and that this manifestation must be in a form of which the human faculties can take cognisance.

But it seems advisable, in view of the actual form which the question assumes within our own experience, to speak in a somewhat fuller way of the relation between that historical Christ, the child of Nazareth, about whom I have been telling my dream, and the eternal Christ, the Divine presence in the world, the expression of the relationship between man and God, the embodiment of the purpose of God and His unending interest in man.

This is the fundamental question which underlies and embraces all other questions regarding Christianity.   It is the answer to this question that divides the schools.   This is the question that forces itself on every one who possesses sufficient intellectual power to think about the nature of the Universe of which he forms a part, the question which every one must put to himself and answer for himself.

With regard to this question two lines of

thought naturally suggest themselves to those
whose life is to a large extent passed amid the
influences of a University ; one historical, the
other literary.

That the Christ must come on earth in
manifest form is, as we have seen, a matter of
necessity.   It must be so, in the nature of
things.   But the answer to this new question
is a matter of historical evidence.   We are
placed in the position of John the Baptist,
when he sent to ask, " *Art thou he that should
come ? or look we for another ?* "

The answer of history is clear and decisive.
The life of Jesus is the knot in which all the
threads of previous history are gathered up,
and from which the threads of succeeding
events again diverge.   In that single figure
all previous development finds its sufficient
explanation.   From that single figure, subsequent development takes a fresh start.

This is not the place, nor is it necessary, to
exhibit in detail the truth of those statements
by showing, even in a brief hurried outline,

how the world was ripe for the perfect idea,
and offered then, and only then, the needed
period of peace for absorbing the teaching of
Christ under the unity of the great Empire,
when the world lay exhausted after the failure
of all other experiments ; and how the cham-
pioning of, or the resistance to, the new
religion of Christ—even in the very imperfect
and inadequate form in which men have as yet
been educated to understand and elevated to
accept it—has impelled and governed all subsequent evolution : the phases of Roman imperial history : the destruction of the Western
Empire by the barbarians : the revival of
Semitic Judaism with some admixture of
Christian ideas unified by the stern spirit of the
desert under the form of Mohammedanism :
the thousand years during which the New
Christian Rome, the capital of the Christian
Empire, saved Europe from the inroad of that
strong revival and gave it time slowly to
assimilate the organisation of the Rome that
it had destroyed : the preservation of ancient

literature and thought and law by the Western Church and the Eastern Christian Empire: the building up of modern society and administration on a broad basis of accumulated experience under Christian forms: the conquest or the absorption of the world by Christianised forms of government.

All that is patent to every one. Men may, from their different points of view, either ridicule or lament the imperfection of the Christian forms in which the best governments and the best societies have as yet been able to clothe themselves. They may inveigh against the evils which are still free to flourish and to spread owing to the too low standard of education and thought and life among even the most advanced nations. But the main facts are undeniable and are not denied. Jesus remade the evolution of history; and those who criticise most severely the contemporary developments of history and life among the Christian nations, reproach them with their failure adequately to comprehend and reproduce His spirit. In other words, Jesus stands forth, even in the estimation of unsympathetic opponents, as the one perfect embodiment of the Divine spirit in human nature.

There remains another point of view from which to approach the question.   St. Paul and St. John have expressed clearly the nature and mutual relations of the two Christs, the eternal Divine presence and the historical figure of Jesus ; and, in describing the former, we have only given a weak paraphrase of some of their impressive words.   They emphatically identify the two figures, and build their life on the identification.   And the authors of the four Gospels unanimously represent the historical Jesus as claiming on many occasions to be the eternal Christ.

In some way the persons who had come most familiarly in contact with Jesus had acquired a belief in this identity ; and the belief reconstituted their mind and nature, and gave them an incomparable influence in human history.   They could not but believe.   They had seen and known. It would have been as easy for them to deny themselves, their existence, their self-identity, as to doubt that the man whom they had known was the Christ. There was no room in their nature for doubt or hesitation. That truth filled up their entire consciousness, and crushed out every other thought. It formed the firm foundation on which their whole life and mind henceforth was built up.

Moreover that belief of theirs formed the foundation on which the whole of modern life has been built up. Alongside of that belief there is in the world no other factor to place. It has influenced almost as profoundly those who stand outside of it, as those who are within its pale. No man can shake it off, or get away from it. It makes his surroundings and moulds his character, guides his education and determines his destiny, in spite of himself.

In ordinary life and in all the business of the world, one of the most valuable qualities that a man can be endowed with is the knowledge of men and of human nature, the insight into character, the ability to judge who is worthy of trust and in what line each can be safely trusted.   That is the quality beyond all others by which the successful men, the men great in practical life, have always been distinguished.   And similarly in historical matters, the student is continually presented with cases of conflict of evidence ; and the question always comes up whom shall he trust, whose evidence can be accepted as really weighty and trustworthy.   He needs that practical discrimination which shall enable him to decide between the honest and the dishonest, between the competent and the incompetent witness.

From this point of view, then, the ultimate question is, can we believe those witnesses?

The verdict of the world, and especially of those who are trained in practical life and in knowledge of men, is beyond all doubt.   Those are trustworthy witnesses.

Especially, the thought that Jesus could have uttered any claim to be what He was not is rejected as inconsistent with His personality.

He could not possibly have been what He was in the world, if He had been capable of entertaining a false thought or compassing an imposture. Such a theory might be entertained by a pedant in his study, but not by a man able to judge of real life.

That verdict is quite apart from any expression of opinion, that the judgment and appreciation and memory of those witnesses were always faultless. It is simply a verdict that they are witnesses of the highest class among human beings.

The supposition either of conscious imposture or of unconscious deception has long been abandoned. No rational being now could hold either, or would waste his time in noticing or refuting either. The world of thought has passed beyond such fancies, though there will always be cases of survival of those and other outworn ideas.

At the present time the problem and the doubt have taken a different form. Since it has proved an untenable and impossible supposition either that Jesus could have made a false claim or that the obviously trustworthy and capable men who lived in His company could have admitted and believed such a false claim, if made by Him, the inference must necessarily be either that the claim was true, or that it was never made at all.

The latter alternative is the one that many modern scholars have adopted. Resolute that such a claim cannot be true, and wrongly branding it as involving an element of the supernatural, they have maintained that Jesus never made any such claim ; that those who knew Him never admitted it ; that it was a delusion of the second century, which grew up in the popular mind spontaneously and without conscious or deliberate fabrication on the part of any one, as the true outlines of the form and teaching of Jesus became blurred in the memory of mankind ; and that the documents, which describe the claim as made by Jesus and believed by His own followers and friends, were written a century or more after His death, and attest, not the facts of the early first century, but the beliefs of the middle of the second century.

That theory, in various slightly differing expressions, has been the central point in the controversies of the last forty years. Its champions naturally attempted to prove their contention by discovering indications of late origin in the books themselves. It is admittedly impossible that books could be written about A.D. 160 without bearing the marks of contemporary thought and of the conditions amid which they were composed ; and the theory of late origin must demonstrate its reasonableness by pointing out the marks of lateness, *viz.*, statements that are out of keeping with the spirit of the first century or views that savour of the second century.

This point it is important to notice. Those scholars did not begin to suspect a late origin for those books on account of the indications which they had detected in them. On the contrary, having for other reasons formed the belief that the books must be incorrect and unhistorical, they framed the theory of their late origin, and then set to work to find in them the required indications of lateness.

The real ultimate cause of their eagerness to discover historical grounds on which to rest their theory lies in their preconceived idea that the Divine nature could not have appeared on the earth in human form—in other words, that the Divine cannot manifest itself to man in a way to be cognisable by human faculties.

But this point is often ignored, whether consciously or unconsciously—probably sometimes consciously, sometimes unconsciously. There are some who, while not merely quite ready to accept, but founding their whole thought and life upon, the view that the Divine nature can manifest itself to man, are yet impressed by the ingenuity and logical skill of the arguments on which the theory of a late origin was supported, and fail to per-

ceive that the theory never had any real
foundation in strict historical investigation,
but was merely an attempt to bolster up a
preconception diametrically opposed to their
own view.

I am not here conducting an argument, but
merely stating impressions ; and therefore I
may plainly and simply express an opinion.

Already that theory has ceased to be regarded as tenable by any properly trained
scholar.   It has been decisively proved that
the books in question could not have been
written in the second century.   But properly
trained scholars are rare ; and the theory has
at present more adherents than it ever had
before.   It has taken possession of the popular
literature to a great extent ; it has caught the
popular ear ; and it not rarely seizes with
compelling interest the mind of some young
scholar—young either in years or in knowledge—and makes him commit himself to
statements which can only seem laughable to
those who know.   I crave pardon for the

strong expression, but there is always a touch of the comic in the attitude of the youthful critic, however much one sympathises with his enthusiasm.

There are also a few fossil scholars, who have learned nothing during the last score of years, and compose verbal variations on the outworn theories of a former age.   It has become a positive craze with them to dissect and chop up literature into fragments ; and in this impossible attempt they have lost all literary sense and historical insight.

But time is on the side of truth.   The popular mind will gradually become disabused of its mistakes.   One must wait patiently. Discoveries, too, will come to demonstrate to all, what is already sufficiently clear to many. But the process of discovery is slow, for the popular taste is not at present eager for it or ready to support the search.

Two fallacies lie at the bottom of this wide-spread acceptance of a false theory.   One is that there must be some truth in an opinion which many scholars have held.   But there are no bounds to the extent to which the thoroughly logical scholar, working in his study, can go wrong, when he starts from false premises.   The sole value of many very learned and ingenious theories is to disprove the premises from which they start ; and that is the case with the theory of second-century origin of the New Testament books.   The first books in which it was proposed had the value of their suggestiveness, honesty, strong purpose and intense belief.   Their authors had struggled a little onward in the path of knowledge, and not wholly astray.   But their ponderous successors have no originality, and their works are among the least valuable productions of the human intellect.

The other fallacy is that that older theory is supported by, and lends support to, a more modern view that the books in question belong to the later years of the first century.   This is a purely irrational and unpardonable error. Any argument which tells in favour of the one view is an argument against the other. If a book suits the conditions and environment of the period A.D. 150-170 it is utterly out of keeping with the circumstances of A.D. 90; and *vice versa*. Those views are mutually destructive.

In one respect the issue of that theory of second-century origin is different from what its originators intended. It was their original intention to show that there was no deliberate falsehood on the part of any one concerned, that the belief in the Divine nature of Jesus had grown up naturally and then the books expressing the belief had naturally resulted from its existence. Thus the books might be honest, though mistaken.

But they have not established the possibility of such blamelessness. The more carefully the books are studied, the more clear does it become that they purport to be written by the eye-witnesses or by persons in the closest relations with the eye-witnesses. It is not the case that this character is given to them only in a superficial way by attaching ancient names, or by inserting some formal claim. The entire expression and spirit of the books are given by authors who write as being in close or immediate relation with the events they describe, and who, without formally claiming that character, assume that their readers know it.

Accordingly the effect of that theory would be to show that those books were deliberate and conscious falsifications, carried out with a skill that is incredible to any one who knows the character of the second century. The theory does not fulfil the conditions laid down by itself for itself at the outset.

The fact is that, while there are many difficulties still unsolved with regard to the books in question, there is no positive theory of date which is not exposed to far greater difficulties than the view that they are genuine works of the period to which they purport to belong. We must stand by the decisive judgment of the world that they are honest ; and the witness that they bear must be accepted.

The conclusion to which all our lines of thought point is that the belief in a Divine Will ruling in and directing the evolution of history logically and inevitably involves the belief that the historical Jesus is the eternal Christ.

To those to whom the belief in a God seems a fallacy of the untrained intellect, which in the educated mind must be refined and melted down into *a something not ourselves that makes for righteousness* or *a larger power which is friendly to mankind*, our conclusion can only seem fanciful and pitiful.

To us, on the other hand, those attenuated phantoms of ideas can only seem ghosts that delude a mind which has fed upon itself, and neglected to keep itself in harmony with the world around, and thus has become unable to grasp the reality concealed behind the phantom.

CHAPTER VIII

EPILOGUE

CHAPTER VIII.

EPILOGUE.

MEN look at facts from different sides, and often fancy they differ in opinion when they are really trying, and trying vainly, to express the same thought. We all see the figure of Christ before us, but we see it dimly and inadequately, for it is distorted to our gaze in the mist of our own poor individuality. But surely we can all agree in recognising the essential nature of that figure, and the truth for which it stands to us. That truth is the gospel of growth and of striving onward towards an ideal beyond us. Freedom of will, truth, knowledge, goodness, beauty, we cannot attain absolutely unto ; they are above us and outside us ; but just as the man who has knowledge is the man who has struggled a little way forward on the road to knowledge, so we make all things ours by believing in them and striving towards them. The good man is he who has tried hard to achieve even a little progress on the way to goodness : he is made good, because he has believed and tried.   And the guarantee that all good things are ours lies in that one supreme Truth, the Life of Christ : we are *justified by Faith.*

But what does that saying of Paul's mean ? Wherein consists the guarantee ?

There is in man the spark of the Divine nature.   We know that, because we see it in Jesus.   He was a man, who by thought, by work, by self-denial, by superiority to all the temptations that tried Him, grew to perfect consciousness of His Divine nature, His mission and His sonship of God.   Human limitations gradually fell away from Him, and in the process of His education " *He increased in favour with God and man* ".   And that word Education expresses the truth to us under another form.   The life of Christ is just the

Education of Christ. His temptations, like ours, came to an end only with His death. In the Garden of Gethsemane occurred His last victory over His last temptation : then and only then His education was completed.

But we cannot of ourselves or through our own power grow into full consciousness of the Divine element within us. The spark of the Divine fire is too feeble in our spirit. *This muddy vesture of decay, which doth grossly close us in*, clings too close and impedes our effort too effectually. No education is enough for us. No man can, by any process of study and meditation and high aims and good works, bring himself into complete sympathy with and understanding of the Divine nature : no man can *by searching find out God.*

Our one and only hope lies in the intensity of our belief that this can be done—in spite of the impossibility—that the Divine element in us can overcome the lower nature, and assert itself in absolute victory, though we cannot ourselves succeed. And we know that it can be done, because Jesus has done it: because He died to prove this truth, and lives to make this truth strong for every man.

This, then, is the faith in Jesus, which Paul has made clear to us. This *cannot* be done by us, and yet it *can* be done: there is the apparent contradiction. Can we believe that it has been achieved by Christ, and that therefore it is possible for us though we cannot ourselves do it? If we can believe that, with all the force of real belief, we have the power of faith, and we receive our inheritance as the Sons of God in Christ.

"Faith"—"Justification by Faith"—"Sons of God"—these and many other terms in the Philosophy, or the Gospel, of Paul are apt to become stereotyped and to lose their meaning for us. There is in them an element of metaphor and parable; and we often hear that element pressed with remorseless thoroughness into rather fantastic forms, which are only veils enveloping and hiding the Truth, while they make its general shape roughly perceptible

to the ordinary mind.   It would be unfortunate that any one should cling to the skirts of
the veil and forget the personality that it hides ;
and it is unfortunate that children, grown too
familiar with those metaphors and wrongly
taking them for realities, fail to learn, when
growing education gives them a more scientific
view and they can no longer be content with
the metaphors, that there is a reality behind
them.

In this education there is necessarily involved a moment of destruction, when the
old idea seems to crumble beneath our feet ;
but it does not really crumble, it is merely
changing its form. We are remaking it for
ourselves by understanding it afresh and
understanding it better. Our error lies in
ignoring the fundamental fact of evolution.
The idea has changed, and yet it is the same :
it has died, that it may live. If we would
only look aright, we should see that the one
figure of Christ still stands before us, the same
Christ that our mothers taught us in infancy ;

and yet, though the same, it has, I think, during the progress of our education, grown in nobility and beauty, and *in favour with God and man*. It is the sum and the quintessence of all our knowledge : it is the expression of all that we have comprehended in the universe.

In one of his most remarkable poems—the "Epilogue," which concludes "Dramatis Personæ"—Browning describes the development of the religious idea, under the form that three speakers successively express their religious feeling.

The first speaker, as David, utters the heart-filling satisfaction of a ceremonial religion, in which the real *presence of the Lord* is veiled in the cloud of symbolism and metaphor amidst those marvellous accompaniments, which primitive thought craves.

> Then the Temple filled with a cloud,
>   Even the House of the Lord ;
> Porch bent and pillar bowed :
>   For the presence of the Lord,
> In the glory of his cloud,
>   Had filled the House of the Lord.

The second speaker, as Renan, stands for the destructive moment. He stands there content and unanticipating, fully satisfied that he has reached the term of perfect knowledge, and that there is nothing to look forward to : he has buried his dead God, and placidly expresses his sentimental regret for the loss of some charming emotions which the dead religion could once evoke. The Face which David saw he can no longer see. There remains no consolation for him except in the consciousness that he has freed himself from mist and cloud and metaphor and miracle, no happiness except in the contemplation of his own hopeless misery, as he stands on the lofty pinnacle of thought to which he has raised himself. He feels an infinite pity for himself, he *looks upon himself and curses his fate*, as he thinks of the awful situation which he is called upon to occupy. Now that the Divine idea in the world has been dethroned, he must himself fill the place, wield the sceptre and wear the crown !

Oh, dread succession to a dizzy post,
Sad sway of sceptre .whose mere touch appals,
Ghastly dethronement, cursed by those the most
On whose repugnant brow the crown next falls.

There is always a certain element of comedy in the attitude of the greater critic, who seems to be saying, "I accept the world and its burden"; and Browning has not failed to appreciate that aspect of Renan's position.

The third speaker has no name. I used to fill the gap with the name of Thomas Hill Green, who about the close of my undergraduate days was giving me eyes and understanding to read the poem; and I used to dream that its origin lay in some conversation of the poet with the philosopher, at the college where the latter was resident and the former an occasional visitor. This third speaker has gone through the first and the second stages of thought, but he has not come to a standstill, like the second speaker : he has perceived that the relation of earth to heaven, of man to God, is real and must be thought out : he will not let you rest until you have found your God again, and seen his Face :

> Witless alike of will and way divine,
> How heaven's high with earth's low should intertwine !
> Friends, I have seen through your eyes : now use mine.

He has seen the dead come to life, for he has *watched when nature by degrees grows alive around him.*   To him there is nothing dead in the world : there is only life and truth.   The old religion has become real to him again, though the ceremonies and symbols no longer cling around it, or hide the real person from him.   And the personality that has emerged from behind the veil is the one truth, the one reality in the world, Christ :

> That one Face, far from vanish, rather grows,
> Or decomposes but to recompose,
> Become my universe that feels and knows.